IMAGE

Chesterfield
1945–1995

'Discover Chesterfield'. 1982 was the centenary of public transport in Chesterfield and the occasion was marked by a procession of old and new buses round the town, including the restored horse-drawn coach (on a suitable trailer). After the parade the vehicles were on show in the Town Hall car parks. This Daimler Fleethire carried a livery depicting much of the refurbishment recently completed in the town.

IMAGES OF ENGLAND

Chesterfield
1945–1995

Roy Thompson

NONSUCH

Front cover illustration: The arches of T.P. Wood's wine and spirit business seen here in 1961 before this building was removed to make room for Littlewood's new store. Wood started his business at this address in 1844, and as it prospered, expanded northwards and built a bottling factory at St George's Works which is now the Co-op electrical deptartment. Besides being Mayor three times Wood was also a generous benefactor to his adopted town. This photograph is used by courtesy of Mr George W. Martin.

First published 1996
This new pocket edition 2006
Images unchanged from first edition

Nonsuch Publishing Limited
The Mill, Brimscombe Port,
Stroud, Gloucestershire, GL5 2QG
www.nonsuch-publishing.com

British Library Cataloguing in Publication Data.
A catalogue record for this book is available from the British Library.

ISBN 1-84588-261-X

Typesetting and origination by Nonsuch Publishing Limited
Printed in Great Britain by Oaklands Book Services Limited

Contents

An aerial view, probably in the 1940s. The camera is looking to the west with the smoke blackened church and spire barely discernible from this angle.

Acknowledgements

My grateful thanks are due to the following for information, assistance and permission to reproduce photographs: Mr Brian Austin, Mr Derek Byfleet and the Gilbert and Sullivan Society, the Staff of the Chesterfield Museum, the Building Control Department of the Borough Council, the Chesterfield Photographic Society, Mrs Winifred Hope, Mr Robert D. Howes, the Staff of the Local History Section, Chesterfield Library, Mr M. Langley, Mr Bernard Marsden, Mr George Martin, Mr Richard A. Matthews, Mr Humphrey Oliver, Management of the Pomegranate Theatre, Mr Wilf Polkinghorne, Mr David Roberts, Mr George Tagg and to my wife for her forbearance, skill and assistance during the preparation of this book. Special thanks also go to Mr Edward Parr for his time and expertise.

Introduction

Progress would be wonderful – if only it would stop!

Changes that occurred in the distant past are often well researched and documented, but the environmental changes of one's lifetime can go unremarked and hardly noticed unless they happen to intrude on one's own habits or interests.

Some of Chesterfield's most significant changes over the last few decades have been in the heavy industries around the town, which once provided employment to many local families and contributed a great deal to the local economy. Iron-making at Sheepbridge, Staveley and Clay Cross, gas and coke manufacture at Staveley, NCB Avenue and the town gasworks have ceased production or closed, resulting in the loss of not only jobs but also other supportive and supply industries. Efforts to find cheaper and more environmentally friendly energy sources have led to the replacement of traditional solid fuels in the home and for industrial processes by gas and electrical power and other 'national influences' have contributed to the loss of local coal-mining and with it a host of traditional local employment opportunities and satellite businesses. All these sad demises have taken their toll of the town's economy, hastening the departure of once-thriving businesses in Chesterfield.

Large chain stores such as Woolworths and Marks and Spencer are still here, of course, having national assets to withstand local recessions, but well respected and once much used locally based department stores like J.K. Swallows and John Turners have closed their doors for the last time to the regret of many in the town.

Many specialist commercial concerns seem to have been forced out of business by the arrival of the huge chain stores, as instanced by the closing of the local family-run ironmongers of Urtons, Dobb's, Britts and Haddingtons, whilst others have ceased trading because of take-overs or closed because of the owner's retirement, like E. Woodhead, Brian English, W.F. Taylor and S.H. Redferns. All of these once well-known firms sold quality provisions for generations. With all these retailers one could buy just as much as one required and not what the modern manufacturers decide you will buy in their pre-packaged items.

National economies and decisions account for many changes and in Chesterfield it has meant the loss of two of its three railway stations: the LDEC passenger line perished in 1957 although the fine station building was used commercially until the site was needed for the AGD complex. The LNER line ceased operations in 1963 and the pretty wooden station was demolished to make way for the new inner relief road.

Chesterfield was once well supplied with breweries, with two of the three main ones surviving the war, but successive takeovers ensured that first, the Brampton, in 1955, and then the Scarsdale in 1959, were eliminated in the face of competition in a harsh commercial climate. As with the brewers, so with many public houses; so many have been lost in the post-war years, in fact, that they could fill a book on their own.

A short count by a native of the town recalled at least twenty-five defunct pubs. Several, like the King and Miller, the Crown, and the Railway Inn, have made way for new development, while others, like the Peacock and the Cavendish, survive but with a new identity.

Television has much to answer for in some aspects of recent change, not least for accelerating the closure of the cinemas in Chesterfield and indeed, the surrounding districts like Hasland, Whittington Moor, New Whittington and Staveley. Town picture palaces Odeon, Regal, Victoria and Corporation Theatre have all been adapted for other uses in post-war years. The Coliseum still stands but there is now no trace of the well-loved Hippodrome which, as the Theatre Royal, also spent several years as a cinema. With the Odeon and Victoria, of course, went two well-patronised dance floors, the only ones remaining in the town after the closure of the Co-operative Hall.

Considerable numbers of dwelling houses have been demolished in the town, mainly to the north and east, to make way for cars, in the form of new roads or parking places. Whole streets and communities have been uprooted and re-housed from these areas as commercial redevelopment has taken place in the southern part of the town.

So far, this brief review has dwelt on demolition and removal, but this is only part of Chesterfield's changes in the post-war years. Although two swimming baths, Markham and Stand Road, have gone, a fine new leisure centre with many excellent facilities now stands in the Queen's Park and a ten-pin bowling alley has arrived at Storforth Lane. A long awaited and excellent museum now lives in the Stephenson Memorial Hall after its vacation by the Public Library, which now occupies the modern, tailor-made building on the site of the old police station. The new Police HQ is now a few yards away along Beetwell Street. Close by is the new shopping arcade, The Pavements, incorporating a supermarket and retaining the original north façade of buildings on Low Pavement.

The new inner relief road is usually full of traffic which would otherwise have clogged up the town centre and three multi-storey car parks and other car parks cater for commuters and shoppers.

New buildings of note include Woolworths and Littlewoods; but the tallest, the AGD tower block, which replaced the LDEC station, is unfortunately reported to have structural problems and is to be replaced by another office block now under construction on Boythorpe Road. Many houses on the new Loundsley Green Estate were built to accommodate the staff of the Post Office Department when it moved to Chesterfield and five hundred local people were recruited to staff this newcomer to the town. Many other new estates, both Council and private, have sprung up on the greenbelt around the town, mainly to the west and north, and the Borough has expanded to include Staveley, boosting the population to over 100,000.

Perhaps the change that has produced the most dramatic alteration in shopping habits in the town has been the establishment of supermarkets in the Borough. There are now five in number and since only one is in the town centre, they put much emphasis on car ownership for shopping and the offer of free parking further encourages shoppers away from the town centre.

It is not the purpose of this book to record the town's history but rather to remind older readers of something they may have forgotten and to show younger ones what was once here. Some items might also amuse the older reader! For example, I suggest they might enjoy trying to identify the odd little features of the town portrayed in Section Seven, before reading the captions.

The task of finding interesting photographs to augment my own quite large collection of this post-war period was not always an easy one (so much gets thrown away!) and I would implore the reader, if he or she has enjoyed this book, never to destroy unwanted family pictures. If you don't want them, give them to the museum and have them preserved for posterity and someone else's pleasure in the future!

One

Town

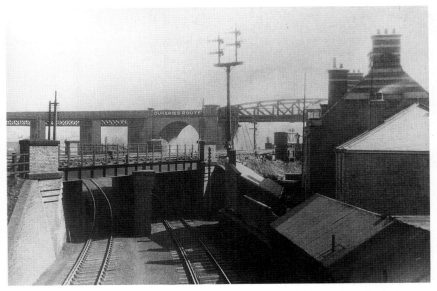

A view along the LNER tracks, well before the closure in 1957 of the Lancashire, Derbyshire and East Coast Railway on the Dukeries route over Horns Bridge. The track between the two was the LMS line which is still in use for the only rail traffic into Chesterfield. The tallest of the buildings on the right is the Horns Hotel, demolished in the 1980s. The M1 feeder roundabout has now taken its place.

What was left of the Horns Bridge complex in the 1980s before the complete removal of the well-known arches. The old road to Hasland was still in use and the present access under the Midland Railway, soon to lead to the M1 at Heath, is in position.

Horns Bridge in the late 1950s or early '60s, as work began on removing the steel span. Everything in this picture has now gone, the bridge, Alma Place terrace and all the houses by the old A61.

Quite a small community disappeared from the bridge area prior to its demolition, not only those on the A61 shown here, but houses and shops in Alma Street, Alma Place, Alma Square and Central Terrace. Almost 120 dwellings were lost in all.

The old Derby Road looking north in the early 1980s, almost ready for the excavators, but not quite. Reeve & Kenning's old workshop still remains, seen here in front of Townrow's Mill.

Lordsmill Street in the late 1970s with a corporation bus carefully easing its way under the Brampton branch bridge. This was the main A61 through the town at that time. All the buildings seen here were removed in the 1980s when this section of road became a cul-de-sac.

From the bridge in the previous photograph the camera now looks south to the new exit to Hasland from the Derby Road, with the old one coned off. New hard-core to the left shows that work has begun on the new relief road here in the early 1980s.

A small terrace south of Hipper Street. These six houses, together with several at right angles to them, were vacated in the late 1970s when this photograph was taken and were soon to disappear before a new commercial block was erected. The footpath to the right of centre went under the Brampton spur embankment to Central Terrace, Horns Bridge and Baden Powell Road.

Hipper Street had already lost several terraced houses when Markham Road was extended, well before the war. These remaining ones in the 1970s had been vacated for demolition, as had the parallel row to the west.

This shows the rear (west) aspect of Hipper Street. There were originally fourteen houses in this terrace north of the new Markham Road on the site now occupied by the police station.

Beetwell Street in the 1970s. The north side had gone and there are temporary shops on the left. All the buildings after the Georgian three-storey terrace were to be removed as far as Hipper Street for the construction of the Police Headquarters.

Lordsmill Street and Beetwell Street in the early 1950s. Everything seen here has now disappeared. The post-war Vauxhall House on the left, a filling station and garage, has made way for the Social Services office and a Bingo Hall. The white, Kenning's parts department building has given way to the Police Headquarters and the old Brampton pub, the Prince of Wales, has gone forever.

The old houses on Lordsmill Street opposite Hollis Lane were pulled down in the 1960s and the site is now a car park, after temporary occupation by portakabin shops. The 1934 bus stand on Vicar Lane survived into the 1990s.

Above: Another Brampton Brewery pub, the Crown, on Lordsmill Street in the early 1950s. Rebuilt by the brewery in 1906 it was closed in 1966 and demolished in 1970. The buildings below, which included a fishing tackle shop and a fish-and-chip shop, went at about the same time.

Left: This narrow lane ran from Beetwell Street to the rear of South Street properties which included the Commercial Hotel and the Bricklayers' Arms. It is thought that the Handyman's Store was one of the first of its kind in Chesterfield, moving to Holywell Street shortly after this photograph was taken at the end of the 1960s.

Beetwell Street from the east in the 1960s. It can be seen that in this area was some of the oldest property in the town, housing long-established businesses; Ellse the pawnbroker, Marshall's fishmongers and Kirk's tinsmiths among them.

Ellse's has gone, as also has Brady the watch repairer, 'Cloggy' Nash and the cycle shop. The Prince of Wales would soon follow.

The demolition team has almost finished off the old bow-front windowed shop of Fred (Pat) Nash, who made clogs here for more than forty years, often helped by characters known as 'Spanish Joe' and 'Little Billy'. Nash lived on Dixon Road and died in 1947, aged 59. His bench and tools are preserved in the Chesterfield Museum.

New Beetwell Street in about 1958, with the old police station on the left, separated from Legard's Leather Stores by Falcon Yard. Legards closed and the shop was demolished for road widening in 1974. The old Court opposite, with the steps leading to the officials' entrance, was removed at about the same time. This building housed the local Petty Sessions for nearly 100 years.

This is a view from the tower of the Parish Church in 1983, looking down on the old British School of Industry, Hollis Lane. Between there and the camera a whole community has disappeared; Station Road, Spa Lane, Eyre Street, Mill Street, including several small shops, the Queen's Hotel and Scarsdale Brewery. The area seen here is now almost wholly occupied by the inner relief road and council car parks.

Above: A last look at the old, complete, Beetwell Street looking east. The bow-fronted shop of 'Cloggy' Nash, the striped barber's pole and a wide variety of old building styles are evident. The date is probably the late 1940s, judging by the lady's dress style.

Left: This grim-looking building was situated in the yard off Beetwell Street before the wholesale clearances of the 1950s and 60s. It had access for vehicles on South Street, between the Commercial Hotel and the Bricklayers' Arms, with pedestrian ways to Vicar Lane and Beetwell Street. Its original use has been difficult to identify, but it may have been a mill operated in the last century by Wm.H. Bannister, 'Corn, flour and oil-cake merchants' of Beetwell Street.

An interesting view, revealed during demolition of a Victorian block of shops which had living accommodation above. The oddly placed west windows reveal the fact that it was built after the smaller property to which it was joined. To the right can be seen the arch to Beetwell Square, from which the photograph on page 68 was taken.

The north side of Beetwell Street at the Lordsmill Street end in about 1958. John Green's had moved here from the Hipper Street corner of Beetwell Street some years earlier. This site, and that of the Prince of Wales on the left, is now a carpark.

Demolition starts on the old garage, *c.* 1982. This building, between the police H.Q. and its charge office, once housed the fire appliances and ambulances, with flats above for police and fire brigade chiefs.

Shuttering and reinforcement for the new library is here in place above ground level in late 1982 and the concrete is soon to be poured in.

Almost ready for the foundations to be laid for the library complex but there is still some way for the excavators to go. This south east corner will eventually contain a below ground lecture theatre and storage areas. At this stage the discovery of several wells and a coal mine entrance caused a six-day extension to the building contract.

The finished library shortly after it was opened, in January 1985, by Mark Fisher MP. Built by Ford and Weston of Derby at a cost of £2.8 million it has a total floor area of over 4,000 sq metres and is air-conditioned throughout. It was designed by the DCC under project architect M. Chapman ARIBA and is the largest library in the county. In 1989 the library issued more than 900,000 books.

A view of a familiar facade in early 1982. Behind the taller block was Theatre Yard, where a playhouse once stood and, later, a yard where firemen drilled with their appliances. To the right is Falcon Yard, by the building used at one time as a charge room by the police.

Low Pavement in the late 1970s, with some once well-known shops now vacated. One plan for the new development called for the removal of most, if not all, of the existing buildings seen here and the covering of the Market Square. After much local discussion the north facades were retained and the prize-winning Pavements mall built behind them.

New Beetwell Street looking east before demolition in the late 1970s. Brayshaw's printing works and the bus shelter conceal a very old byway, Wheeldon Lane, running from the market toward the River Hipper. The new road level, crossing the old one, necessitated steps on either side leading down to Markham Road.

A photograph taken about 1982 from almost the same viewpoint as the one above. There has been quite a change on both sides of New Beetwell Street – look at the price of petrol at Portland Garage!

What was left of the old police and fire station in the early 1980s, exposing a view to the rear of South Street.

The west end of New Beetwell Street in the mid-1970s from the south. All the buildings on Low Pavement have lost their south facings and are now conjoined with the Pavements complex. The exception is the Peacock Inn which has been tastefully restored as the Peacock Centre.

Low Pavement from the south before demolition. The direction of the successive additions to these properties reflects the many north to south yards running downhill.

The same scene as above with the removal of Low Pavement under way in the area now occupied by the Somerfield supermarket.

Mason's buffet on the corner of Tontine Road, opposite the East Midland bus station. It was still refreshing the traveller and others in the 1970s, just as it had been doing since wartime days, but it would not do so for much longer.

The popular tea bar has gone, also the Kirk building, and the rear of Greaves' chemist and the rest will soon follow. The bit of Tontine Road that can be seen in this picture is now the delivery entrance to the Pavements Centre and the Central Library.

The old Chesterfield Workhouse, built in 1763 and just south of the bowling green. It was pulled down shortly after the war. The gable at right angles to it, housed the offices and living quarters of the supervisors. The old slipper baths, now a craft workshop, can be seen on the right.

In 1913 Alderman G.A. Eastwood gave this Hasland park his name and presented it to the town in memory of his late father, Alderman F. Eastwood. The fountain to the right is seen here in its original setting but has now been erected in the south-west corner of New Square in the town centre.

South Street in 1973. The taller buildings were brought down and rebuilt up to the Falcon colonnade and the other shops refurbished. Britt's ironmongers ceased trading in 1988 after over 150 years.

The Red Lion on Vicar Lane which may soon be removed for a proposed development. When local man, Joe Davis, won the World Billiards Title in 1928 he was met at the railway station by a crowd of 5,000 people, some of whom then proceeded to the Red Lion for a celebration. The Vicarage, demolished in the 1980s, can be seen on the right.

Vicar Lane, c. 1975. The corporation Omnibus Station, built in 1934 for services mainly to the south and east of the town, disappeared in the early 1990s. The three-storey house seen on the left was once the residence of one of the owners of nearby Scarsdale Brewery, which later became the brewery office. It was restored privately in the late 1980s.

The south entrance to the tunnel of the Chesterfield loop line in the 1970s and something of a rubbish dump. The faint circle seen below the Hollis Lane bridge is the exit below Brewery Street, just before the station.

These houses on Spa Lane, Station Road corner, appear to have been built on much earlier foundations and were occupied until the middle 1950s when they were demolished. The old labour exchange, left, is presently (1996) being refurbished but the rest of this site is still a parking area.

These houses were opposite Scarsdale Brewery entrance in Spa Lane in 1958. The windows on the right faced onto Mill Street and had a view of the Midland Railway. The van on the far right is parked in front of the Hourglass Inn.

Spa Lane, c. 1962. These houses are now gone but the cast-iron scotches, embedded in the gutter to rest cart wheels against, may still be seen. This picture also provides a rare view of a part of the Hourglass Inn, a Brampton house which closed in 1961. The LNER tunnel ran under the rear of the pub and a 30ft wide ventilation shaft occupied most of the garden. This is a car park now.

The British School of Industry lay on Hollis Lane, once an ancient road to Calow. The school was built in the 1840s as a private school but was later used for many other purposes, including a dance hall, after Hipper Street school was opened in the 1880s. Hollis Nook, the Midland line and Markham's works can be seen beyond the school.

Left: This seventeenth-century, possibly earlier, building, the Falcon Inn, shown here in the early 1980s, has been variously known as a coaching inn, the Falcon Temperance Cafe, Everest Dining Rooms and Boden's Restaurant. It thrived under Bodens from pre-war days to the 1980s, serving mainly fish and chips, on three floors and in a restaurant down Falcon Yard. In 1996 it houses one of the many building society offices in the town.

Below: The east side of the Market Place in the 1960s, with Boots on the corner, the Home & Colonial grocery shop and the Cathedral Vaults all occupying century-old properties. The Cathedral Vaults, known as 'Pretty Windows ' because of its stained glass, were demolished, with some haste, in the 1970s and a more modern version built to replace it, now the Britannia Building Society.

Station Road in the 1970s. These five houses are all that remains of a row extending to Spa Lane and built in the nineteenth century. Some even older terracing had already gone from the other side. The *Derbyshire Times* offices had been refurbished and extended on the left of the picture. Two other detached houses once stood where the car is parked.

The north end of Station Road, *c.* 1977. Shentall's warehouse (extreme right) had extended towards the louvred cold storage of Warner's fish business on the ground where once stood 'Poor Folks Fold' and Smith's Yard. The old labour exchange can be seen between Warner's and the White Swan Yard. A large air-raid shelter stood in the open space in wartime.

The Heathcote home in 1990 after the demolition of Shentall's warehouse and before the erection of St Mary's Court. Used by the Heathcote family, possibly Chesterfield's most eminent, the house became a school in the 1830s and was Shentall's offices before its present use as a restaurant. The Heathcote family included two Lord Mayors of London and a Mayor of New York.

The junction of Corporation Street with Eyre Street about 1977. The three pillars bar the old way to the station and long before that, to the Bishop's Mill below Tapton. The cars are parked on the site of eighteen dwellings, three shops and the Midland Hotel.

Freeman's Temperance Commercial Hotel, Corporation Street, in the late 1970s. Built in the nineteenth century to attract the rail travellers, this hotel was advertised as 'home from home', with fourteen en suite rooms, billiards and dining saloons. It was Jay's furniture store for some time after the war but stood empty for a long time before its final demolition.

A view of the station goods yard in the 1970s, with Freeman's Hotel prominent, the *Derbyshire Times* Works and the (then) Clifton Hotel visible on either side. The stone building on the right is thought to have been the old Midland Station and is now a smart new office.

A maze of scaffolding that was seen for a time on High Street in the 1980s, as Marks & Spencer was extended and the old corner opposite refurbished for new occupiers following Boots move to Low Pavement.

A relic of the first gas lighting in the town by Joseph Bower in 1824. This lamp standard originally stood in the south-east of the Market Place, supplied with gas made by Bower in his workshop beneath the Cathedral Vaults for 'seven pounds per season'. It is shown here in the 1950s on Packers' Row (left) and in its new home in St Mary's churchyard.

The site between Burlington Street and Church Lane in 1975. Woolworths was demolished and a new store erected, the upper storey going over Church Lane and almost to Vicar Lane. At this stage, a large stone-lined shaft was uncovered at the south-east corner of the old store, revealing other previous developments.

A view through the Shambles in the 1970s, with almost the only surviving parts of the original stalls on the left. The well-known chip shop is still there although now with a 'closed' notice on the window. Stanley Shackleton's hairdressing salon is on the right, now a part of Lloyd's bank.

Left: This long, north to south, section of the Shambles is now called Palmersgate. The photograph was taken about noon, which is the only time of day that these old yards get full sunlight, in 1977 just prior to the refurbishing of the area. The old chip shop is on the right, and Boden's Restaurant can be seen on Low Pavement.

Below: Excavations for the extension to the Market Hall in 1978. The refurbishment of the Low Pavement properties has also started, but the removal of the old underground public toilets has not yet been completed.

In the 1960s the market square was cleared of stalls to permit free parking. The market hall has yet to get its cupola and the new NatWest bank is under construction.

Taken from the upper deck of a Corporation bus on a market day in the early 1970s, this view shows the main road passing through New Square. The NatWest bank and the shops below are now in business and the stalls are busy too. The market hall once housed the Post Office in the corner seen here in shadow.

The date of this photograph is not known but it may have been a record taken before demolition in the 1950s. The inn closed in February 1937, its licence being transferred to the Walton Hotel by the licensees, Scarsdale Brewery. It was owned at that time by Dents, who purchased the inn, stables and five dwelling houses at an auction held in 1926 at the Portland Hotel. The premises were leased by Duncan Gilmour Ltd.

The Star and Garter Yard in the late 1940s or early 1950s. Access was not only from New Square but also from West Bars, between Urtons ironmongers and a newspaper shop next to Dents old premises.

The west end of West Row in the 1950s. These solid-looking terraced houses dating, probably, from the early 1800s ran from the middle of West Bars to Boythorpe Road. They were demolished in the 1960s and a multi-storey car-park now stands on the site.

Left: The fine terminus of the Lancashire, Derbyshire & East Coast Railway in the late 1950s. The trains had stopped running in March 1957. The offices were used for a time by Credlands and also Birtley Engineering but the building had gone by the early 1960s to make way for the extension of West Bars and the AGD complex.

Below: The Post Office Accountant General's Department came to Chesterfield in 1963. Chetwynd House, named after Geo. Chetwynd, head of the AGD in Gladstone's time, became the largest building in the town at 92ft 9in high and built at a cost of £1.34m. It housed 1,600 staff of whom 900 moved from the previous department in London and were housed in 'luxury council houses and flats' mostly on Loundsley Green. The complex included a library and cinema on the upper storeys and the canteen was described as 'like a high class cabaret club'. The east side is seen sheeted and scaffolded in 1995 for repair work to maintain the fabric before the building is vacated for new accommodation on Boythorpe Road.

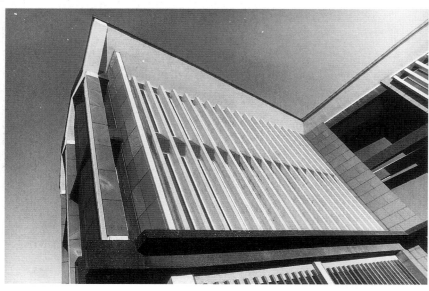

Chesterfield Courthouse in 1970. A radical design by Professor J.S. Allen, it was built at a cost of £200,000 by local contractor Thomas Beighton to replace the old Municipal Hall on Beetwell Street used as a court for nearly 100 years. Housing four courts, offices and cells, it was opened by Lord Denning, Master of the Rolls, in September 1965.

Brampton Brewery in 1980. Brewing had taken place on this site since the early 1800s but this building dates from 1905, when it became the first electrically operated brewery in the country, owning and supplying 140 pubs and outlets. Successive takeovers left the company with Courage Ltd, and the last brew was made on 15 June 1955. The B & Q store now occupies the site following demolition in 1984.

This property stood on the south side of Chatsworth Road between Tap Lane and the corner of Wheatbridge Road for over a century and comprised several small shops among the cottages, including the long-established business of Nicholson's, hairdresser.

This curiously shaped building stood at the junction of Chatsworth Road and Old Road until demolition in 1971 for road improvements. A private house in the last century it has been a post office and a doctor's surgery and was used as a police station by the Corporation until 1930.

The rear of the old police station in the 1970s. A new road has been made on the site of the old school and the island takes shape. The building with the single chimney on the site once housed the local fire appliance.

Chatsworth Road as it was in the 1960s with two-way traffic and the start of demolition on the island. St Thomas' school was 100 years old and although it closed as a school in 1929 it was used for church purposes for a number of years.

Markham swimming baths photographed c. 1960, was given to the town by C.P. Markham. These baths were well-used by a couple of generations of swimmers, despite the smuts emanating from nearby chimneys! It was closed in the 1970s after the opening of a fine new leisure centre in the Queen's Park.

Beaver Place between Factory Street and Shepley Street was a pleasant looking enclave of cottages when this photograph was taken in 1988. In the nineteenth century this small area was known for felting rabbit and other fur to make gentlemen's tall hats known as Beavers. These houses vanished in the early 1990s.

Red Row, Brampton in the 1970s, stood between Heaton Street and Victoria Street parallel to Chatsworth Road. It was removed in the 1970s and replaced by small bungalows when much of this area was redeveloped.

Victoria Drill Hall, Ashgate, photographed in 1980. Named to honour the Queen's Diamond Jubilee it was officially declared open by Field Marshall Lord Roberts of Waterford and Kandahar (a Boer War hero) on 28 September 1898. The hall lasted almost 100 years, housing meetings, concerts, boxing matches, dinners and dances, long after the drill hall function ceased. It was demolished in the 1980s.

Elder Way in the late 1940s, and nearly deserted too! The war interrupted the Chesterfield Cooperative Society's development plans and the spaces either side remained vacant throughout the war and until the Coop resumed its expansion in the late 1950s and again in the 1980s.

The same view as above in 1976. The Coop has here reached Saltergate and the bus terminus has developed.

Saltergate, *c.* 1948, when there were shops to the left, then almshouses, a hairdresser, Graham More, the *Star* offices, Fish the furrier, the tripe shop and others. All are now gone, including the old Staffordshire Farmers' offices on the right, by the Ashgate bus stand.

The two old plane trees had to go, being a dangerous hazard to the Corporation Guy double-deckers. The entrance leading to the Elder Yard Chapel is almost all that remains of Saltergate between Elder Way and Broad Pavement.

The Royal Hospital in the 1970s. It began life in 1859 as the Chesterfield and North Derbyshire with just twelve beds, growing as local benefactors supported the addition of new wards. Eventually it outgrew itself when acres of space around it became passageways between new buildings and departments. The main 1859 building remained empty for some years after the hospital transferred to Calow in the 1980s and was then tastefully renovated to become Kennings headquarters in the 1990s.

The hospital shell in the early 1990s. A new roof is under construction and most of the outbuildings have gone to make car parking space.

All that remained of Shepleys Yard in 1977. To the left can be seen temporary portakabin shops. The site was cleared soon after this time for Comet and other stores on Saltergate and Broad Pavement.

Looking west from Felkin Street in the early 1980s. These once elegant dwellings are abandoned on Durrant Road and Tapton Lane and, together with the sweet factory and nearly forty other houses, would soon go for the construction of the inner relief road.

Brewery Street, *c.* 1981. These houses, once overlooking the GC station, are here empty and awaiting demolition.

Rather more handsome residences compared with the terraces higher up Brewery Street but with Willett's shop, offices and sweet factory they disappeared before the by-pass construction. The wall on the right was the bridge parapet over the railway line.

Infirmary Road in 1981. Only the base of the pretty wooden station building remains in the way of the new road which follows the GC route at this point after bisecting Corporation Street.

A view of the Tapton Lane area in August 1982 taken from Theatre Lane, where brambles proliferated, on the way leading to the old Hippodrome stage doors. The car is parked where once stood the Railway Inn which went in 1961, and the large Cabinet Works of Eyres extended as far as Parker's Yard, below the Odeon Cinema.

A train just leaving the Great Central LNER platform in 1960, with the engine shed (left) and the Technical College to the right. This loop left the main line at Heath and rejoined it at Staveley.

The remains of the station in about 1963, with the new Brewery Street bridge in position.

This photograph was taken in the 1970s from Infirmary Road, opposite the GC station and looking south along the loop tunnel (see page 31 for the other end). The first arch seen is the bridge over Brewery Street and it is just possible to see the Hollis Lane exit, right of centre.

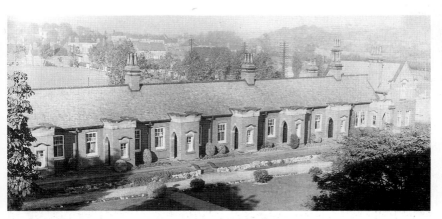

The eight 'Eventide Homes for Gentlewomen', photographed from the chemistry laboratory of the Technical College in 1952. These Accrington brick dwellings, built by William Rhodes, were the gift of Alderman Edward Eastwood in 1908 for 'aged gentlewomen of some slight means'. They had to provide their own furniture. The buildings had gone by the mid-1970s.

Dunston Lane in the 1940s before big developments took place in this area in the 1950s and 60s. The war postponed further building after the houses near to Newbold Road junction had been completed.

The Ashgate Hospice began its work of respite care for the terminally ill in 1988, building accommodation for in-patients and day patients to the east of the old Barnes residence at Ashgate, which is used for administration purposes. The permanent staff comprises two resident doctors, including a Medical Director and about thirty trained nurses. Other doctors support the hospice and many volunteer helpers give valuable assistance.

Two

Commercial

New Square, until the late '70s, was divided by the main road and bus route from the west end of town. Once known as Swine's Green, a pig market, it was well provided for with hostelries on three sides with the Star and Garter, the Peacock and the Market Hotel. Only the last has survived.

Swallows department store in the 1960s. J.K. Swallow began trading on Burlington Street, before 1870, as an outfitter and clothier. He moved to larger premises opposite, on the north side, expanding around two corners and in 1930 rebuilt in the mock-Tudor style seen here. A popular shop for all kinds of clothing and hardware it closed down in 1970 and the site was redeveloped.

The south side of the market hall in the 1940s, with Mart's gent's hairdresser and Stan Miles, newsagent, either side of the entrance. Next to Miles was Johnsons the arts shop, which moved to West Bars before refurbishment of the building.

John Turner's, seen here in the early 1980s, had been trading in drapery and clothing since 1845. The south-facing side was redeveloped in fashionable mock-Tudor style in the early 1930s, including the landmark garret corner. This shop was well-known in the town for its fascinating overhead wooden-ball money conveyers which carried cash to a central cashier. The business ceased trading in 1987 after an earlier takeover by Courtaulds.

The north side of the market hall in the 1940s, with some well-known names over the shops; Ford's bookshop, and Mason's tobacconists are prominent, Dr Scholl's foot-care shop can be seen too. The hall door, by the nearest car, was once the Post Office and those words can still be seen, though now painted over. The Medical Aid Society occupied the office in the 1940s.

Founded in Liverpool in 1844, Woodheads began in Chesterfield in the 1860s, directly opposite this site on the corner occupied by Collingwoods. This photograph was taken in the 1970s. The store shown was built in 1898 and initially included a very popular billiard room. The firm also ran the Burlington Café on Packer's Row and several outlying branches. The building was taken over by Fine Fare Ltd in the 1960s.

The corner of Burlington Street and Cavendish Street in the late 1940s included multiple stores like Currys, Davys and the Strand Library (2d per book per week) and local firms like Voce and Tinleys. Singer's still occupy the corner site (left), and the overhead showroom of Jas. Woodhouse, high above the pavement, are an interesting reminder of the days when passengers on the upper decks of slow-moving trams were catered for.

Right: Abraham Greaves established this family business in 1836 on Low Pavement, and by 1914, they were not only dispensing chemists but 'suppliers of paint and varnishes, oil and colour merchants' and even supplied collieries and quarries with explosives. The site is now occupied by Boots, and Greaves moved to Vicar Lane in the 1970s. The curious tax-avoiding long window is represented in the new building, as the original is now in the care of the museum.

Below: Once there were three similar colonnaded buildings in the market square. This is the only remaining original, now an arcade entrance to the Pavements. Familiar names in this 1970s picture are; Masons the bakers, Kirks the pork butchers. Sharps wallpaper shop once sold toys and had a café above.

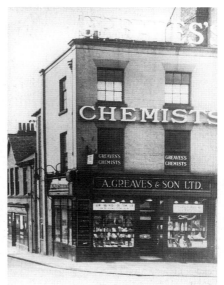

Left: A view of West Bars in the 1950s, clearly taken from atop the market hall tower, showing several features which are now absent. Dents old shop, once occupied by Proctor's florist, opposite, and the shops beyond, also the LDEC station and its goods yard, currently the site of the Postal Finance Department can all be seen. Lower right is the well-known 'spectacle' window of A.V. 'Sandy' Smart, who ran Dent's optician's department.

Below: John Dent began trading in New Square as a dispensing chemist in the early part of the century and also practised as an optician, herbalist and veterinarian. He purchased the Star and Garter in 1926 and died three years later. The business prospered and expanded to include a branch in Newbold. When redevelopment became necessary temporary accommodation was set up alongside it, until the new building was complete in 1962.

Ready for the opening of Dent's temporary shop in 1960 are, left to right: Michael Langley (now a director), Barbara Swain, Wilf Marsden, Cecil White, Anne Still and Mark Evans, manager and director.

These two shops, shown here in about 1970, flourished for many years at the foot of South Street. Legards was the first to go in the 1970s and the building removed for road widening, but Britts lasted until 1988, after which the old shop became a short-lived licensed bar called The Eagle.

The junction of Saltergate and Holywell Street, c. 1960. J.W. Damm's fruit and vegetable shop was there before 1870, as was the Shakespeare where, it is said, was pulled the last pint of Brampton Ale in 1955.

An enlarged detail from a photograph showing the remains of Holywell Street in the 1970s, just prior to removal. The furthest shop was the first business opened by Montague Burton (Meshe David Osinsky) in 1904, who paid rent for it to J.W. Damms, as well as borrowing from him to buy stock. Burton lodged at No.1 Saltergate and later Spencer Street. He later opened the second part of his future empire at nearby Mansfield.

Brian English at his counter in the Chatsworth Stores in Brampton in the last weeks before his retirement in 1996. This high class family grocers business, on the corner of Heaton Street, provided generations with personal service. Many of the fixtures and fittings of the shop have been acquired by Chesterfield Museum for future display.

Goodwin's shop on West Bars, between Foljambe Road and Rutland Road dates back to pre-war days. It lasted until the late 1980s when the three shop frontages were, one by one, occupied by other businesses. This picture was taken in 1950.

Beetwell Street in the 1970s showing the row of temporary accommodation for traders displaced during various contemporary developments. The photograph was taken just before the south side was dismantled, from a position which is now the entrance to the police station.

Wragg's motorcycles business in 1987. The Sheffield based firm took over the Jervis Bros' motor-cycle concern at Horn's bridge in the 1960s and moved to the old Victoria building on Whittington Moor. They had ceased trading by the early 1990s.

Three

Industry

A long-established manufacturer of confectionery, Willetts, who were here in the 1930s, were obliged to move from this Tapton Lane site for road expansion in the 1980s. They have relocated their wholesale business in Whittington Moor.

The mighty gas engines at the Staveley Coal and Iron Co. were the largest in the country. There were three engines with two cylinders each of nearly five feet in diameter. They used waste gas from the four blast furnaces and generated 5,000 kw each at the thirty feet, one hundred ton flywheels. The alternating current was at thirty cycles, and distributed not only for works purposes but to many homes in Hollingwood and Barrow Hill. After leaving the engines the hot gases passed through boilers, raising steam for the works, and then were further used in nearby chemical processes. Installed by Cockerills of Belgium in 1928, the engines worked until the gas supply ceased on closure of the blast furnaces in 1966.

A photograph full of atmosphere and showing the blast furnace plant on the Devonshire
Works of the Staveley Co. in 1949. Four workmen leave the canteen with their tea-cans. All the
structures in this picture had gone by the time the company – then Staveley Chemicals – was
taken over in the 1980s. The works is now owned by the French giant, Rhône-Poulenc.

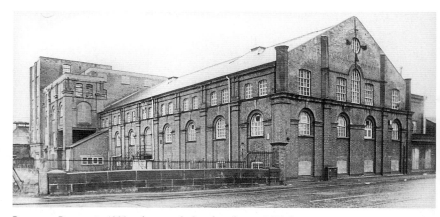

Brampton Brewery in 1980, a few years before demolition. A B&Q superstore now occupies this site. After brewing ceased in 1955 the premises housed only the office and maintenance workers for some time until the Sheffield provisions firm of Nichols acquired the freehold. Auto Windscreens began operations here too for a while, but then moved to the Storforth Lane trading estate.

A rare Transunited bodied SD42/3 Crossley coach in Hulley's livery waiting, in the 1940s, on New Beetwell Street at the Wheeldon Lane stop, adjacent to Brayshaws printing works. Hulleys relinquished family ownership in 1978 to Silver Service, but the name has recently been revived.

Above: The Brampton Brewery offices in 1980, with an Auto Windscreens lorry delivering outside the colonnaded shop. Office equipment was sold here for some years before demolition.

Right: All that remained of the other gas works in 1982. A small plant, it was built by the Midland Railway to supply gas for lighting their nearby signals and station. Gas could also have been supplied to adjacent tanneries in the area, where copious supplies of water were available from the river Hipper. Townrow's mill can be seen behind the site which today is occupied by a furniture store.

The offices of the Chesterfield Gas and Water Board in the late 1960s, stood on the corner of Foljambe Road and Chatsworth Road and replaced an older building which had been there since 1825. This handsome block was removed following the supply of North Sea gas in the 1970s.

The printing presses of the *Derbyshire Times* in the 1970s, when it was a broad-sheet newspaper. The paper was founded in 1854 by Francis A. Hatton and was printed in Angel Yard, off Packers' Row, until moving to Station Road in 1857.

Above: The Shakespeare Inn, seen here around 1970, was built in the 1860s. It boasted a gas-lit skittle alley and was rebuilt by the Brampton Brewery in 1906 in a style that anticipated the half-timbered Chesterfield fashion of the 1930s, making it stand out against the older adjacent properties. The pub was selling Barnsley Bitter when it finally closed, to make a car park, in 1973.

Right: Not all commerce was centred in the town. The Staveley Co., with its furnaces and coke ovens, had a beer licence in order to satisfy thirsts in this hot environment. Here, a group enjoy their pints in front of a mess room decked out for Christmas.

The 1889 water-tower at Robinson's Wheatbridge Works finally had its day in December 1995 when it was pulled down during site clearing for a retail industrial park. To the right can be seen the new PFD building under construction.

A landmark on the road to Staveley for over forty years, this giant concrete cooling tower at Devonshire Works was demolished in the 1980s.

Four

Leisure and Sport

There can be few more pleasant places for an enthusiast to watch cricket than in these leafy surroundings at the Queen's Park, although opportunities have been regrettably few in number now that the policy of the County Club is to play mostly at Derby. Here Derbyshire are playing Yorkshire in the 1970s.

Chesterfield Football Club was a force to be reckoned with in the immediate post-war years, achieving fourth place in the second division. This is a team from that period, left to right, rear: S. Goodfellow, G. Milburn, W. Leivers (?), R. Middleton, K. Booker, W. Kidd, O. Thompson. Front: T. Lyons, -?-, T. Swinscoe, ? Wilson, W. Linacre.

Another CFC team from a little later than the one above, left to right, rear: K. Booker, W. Linacre, S. Milburn, S. Goodfellow, G. Milburn, R. Cushlow, R. Middleton, W. Kidd, -?-, -?-, W. Whittaker. Front: J. Hudson, D. Milligan, T. Swinscoe, ? Wilson, H. Roberts.

The club won the Fourth Division championship in season 1969-70. Here are players of that period, left to right, rear: K. Randall, E. Moss, C. Bell, A. Stevenson, M. Wright, A. Phelan, T. Fenoughty, K. Tiler. Front: K. Stott, J. Archer, D. Pugh, D. Wilson, P. Cliffe, A. Holmes.

During the Festival of Britain in 1951, matches with continental teams were arranged as part of the celebrations. This is a photograph of Chesterfield entertaining Anderlecht of Belgium. Chris Marron is heading goalwards, with Fred Capel in support. Chesterfield won 3-1.

The Old Cestrefeldians took their football seriously in the 1950s and this photograph shows members out training on the Somersall playing field of the school (then on Sheffield Road). Identified are ex-CFC's Billy Kidd (trainer) and the three leading players are Alan Lewis, Ron Lowe and Bill Barnett. The tall goalkeeper at the rear is Bob Howes.

A Staveley works team played friendly matches in 1949 and a team is shown here on the Middlecroft school ground, left to right: J. Randall, B. Stoppard, R. Thickett, J. Mitchell, F. Burnage, R. Harvey. Front: -?-, J. Morris, W. Thornewill, C. Stevenson, A. Savage.

The playbill for the first production at the new Civic Theatre in 1949. There was a resident repertory company of some twenty players and two producers, staging a different production each week. The cast for *See How They Run* included Diana Fairfax, Dera Cooper, Adrian Cairns, Josephine Laurie, Douglas Malcolm, Lewis Wilson, Peter Sallis, Robert Sewell and John York. It was produced by Lawrence Hayes.

First Performance at The Civic Theatre, Monday, 21st February 1949.

CIVIC THEATRE
CHESTERFIELD

Licensee & Manager: Ian Vogler, The Clifton Hotel, Chesterfield

Chesterfield Civic Theatre Limited
(in association with The Arts Council of Great Britain) has
pleasure in announcing the First Presentation to mark the

OPENING
of the Civic Theatre

Commencing **Monday, 21st February**
for one week,

The Funniest Farce of all!

"SEE HOW THEY RUN"
BY PHILIP KING

From the Comedy Theatre, London

PRODUCED BY LAWRENCE HAYES

Monday
to Friday
at 7·0 p.m.
●
Saturday
at 4·30 p.m.
and
7·30 p.m.

Prices of
Admission

Stalls
4/- and 2·6
Reserved

Pit 1·6
Unreserved

Circle
4/- and 2·6
Reserved
1·6
Unreserved

BOX OFFICE OPEN DAILY
From Monday, 7th February onwards   10 a.m. to 7·30 p.m.
SUNDAYS EXCEPTED   TELEPHONE 2901

Applications for Seats by post must be accompanied by stamped addressed envelope
Special concessions for party bookings   Permanent reservations available

FULLY LICENSED BAR

Chesterfield Borough Council   Derbyshire County Council

Thomas Bradshaw Ltd., Marsden Street, Saltergate, Chesterfield.

CHESTERFIELD CIVIC THEATRE
In association with the Arts Council of Great Britain.

OPENING CEREMONY

SATURDAY, 19th FEBRUARY, 1949
at 7·30 p.m.

To be performed by
MISS KATHLEEN HARRISON
(An Artiste of the J. Arthur Rank Organisation)

Chairman: HIS WORSHIP THE MAYOR OF CHESTERFIELD
(Alderman Edgar Smith, D.C.M.).

Ceremonies of Dedication
by

Mr. LLEWELLYN REES
Drama Director of the Arts Council of
Great Britain.
21st February

Introduced by
Councillor J. H. Hodkin

Mr. PHILIP KING
Author of " See How They Run."
22nd February

Introduced by
Councillor E. Swale

Mr. ANDRÉ VAN GYSEGHEM
Director of The Nottingham Playhouse.
23rd February

Introduced by
Mr. Wm. C. Coxall

Mr. E. MARTIN BROWNE
Director of The British Drama League.
24th February

Introduced by
Mr. H. Mellor, M.A.

Dr. L. du GARDE PEACH, M.A., PH.D.
Dramatist and Director of the Great Hucklow Theatre.
25th February

Introduced by
Miss P. M. Wildin

Miss FREDA JACKSON
Renowned Actress of Stage and Screen.
26th February

Introduced by
Mr. L. Lodge, M.A.

The Civic Theatre, now renamed the Pomegranate, staged plays and other shows before its conversion to the cinema, the 'Corporation Theatre' in 1910, with rear projection from the back of the stage. Kathleen Harrison, who opened the theatre, lived to be more than 100 years old.

A Christmas production at the 'Civic', *When Knights Were Bold* with Rowena Ingram, James Belchamber, Pauline Brailsford, Peter Sallis and Phyllida Breaks.

This staging of *Treasure Island* starred Bernard Archard as Long John Silver and Phyllida Breaks as Hawkins.

A popular production in December 1951 was *Charley's Aunt* featuring, left to right: Margaret Tyzack, Anthony Millican, James Belchamber, Alan Rowe and Maureen O'Reilly.

At the Civic Theatre, during breaks by the repertory company, local societies put on some very successful shows. Here is a scene from the Chesterfield Gilbert and Sullivan Society's 1992 production of *Patience* with, left to right: Brian Key, June Geeves, Mike Spriggs, Sue Key and David Stokes.

Above: The Gilbert and Sullivan Society was founded in March 1971 and now has over seventy members. The Society has performed 154 concerts and staged sixteen full stage productions and, in so doing, has raised more than £30,000 for local and national charities. The photograph shows the leads in *The Pirates of Penzance* in 1985, left to right, rear: Mike Spriggs, Lawrence Crick, Brian Key, and Albert Thomas. The ladies: June Geeves, Jackie Boot, Brenda Morton, Elizabeth Jepson and Lynne Patrick.

Opposite above: Adult education in the 1970s. Many schools in the area run non-vocational classes in the evenings and on Saturdays, using part-time tutors under the auspices of the Local Education Authority. Subjects are almost endless, from swimming to flower-arranging. Here, Christine Bimpson re-upholsters a chair at the Peter Webster school, then a full-time A.E. Centre.

Opposite below: Another class at Peter Webster's school, this time photography. In this portrait session the model was Louise Grey who became a successful beauty queen, winning many titles and appearing in the Miss Universe contest in America.

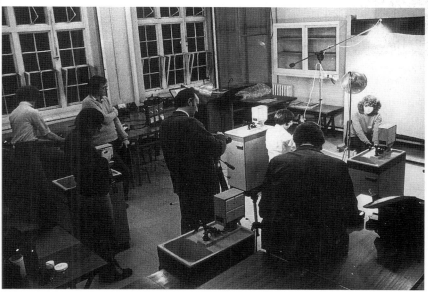

Left: At the time of writing, Chesterfield does not possess a cinema. Here is the old Coliseum, said to have been one of the first permanent cinemas in 1907, in the Central Hall, a disused Methodist Church. Customers could still sit on the old pews in the 1930s, but refurbishment following a fire in 1939 resulted in a comfortable 600-seat theatre and it survived, usually on second-run films, until October 1957. The last film shown was *High Society*. This view was taken in the 1970s during the conversion of the building to a car sales showroom.

Below: The Odeon, as many readers will remember it, (unless they were shown to a seat behind one of the pillars!) with the Pan curtains and the pastoral proscenium arch. Opening as the Picture House in 1923 it was re-named the Odeon in 1938. It survived the television age and finally closed in October 1981. With it went a popular ballroom and restaurant. Refurbishment to the 'Winding Wheel' began in 1987.

Five

People and Events

Roy Cooper, Borough Librarian, photographed just after his retirement in 1974. Born in the town in 1916, Roy was educated at Chesterfield Grammar school and joined the library service in 1935, qualifying as an ALA. After war service in the Far East with REME he became assistant librarian and then Borough Librarian in 1972, retiring with a deserved reputation as a local historian. He was the author of the popular *Book of Chesterfield* (Barracuda Books 1977) and contributed to the publication of the first two volumes of the town's official history. Roy died suddenly in December 1987.

Left: Hiram Tagg, Mayor of Chesterfield in 1957. Born in 1901, Hiram Tagg became a miner at Grassmoor and was one of only four survivors of the tragic explosion in 1933. He was elected to the Borough Council as a Labour member in 1938 and served continuously until his death in 1963, latterly being elected an Alderman of the Borough and Mayor in 1957. He was a keen bandsman in his earlier days, playing with the Salvation Army, the Sheepbridge Silver Prize Band and the Territorial Army Band. He was responsible for many housing reforms in the Borough.

Below: The presentation to the Borough of a seat commemorating the long service on the council of Alderman Hiram Tagg, who died in 1963. The photograph shows Mrs Tagg handing over the seat to the Mayor, Mrs A. Collishaw, in 1966.

Right: In 1995 the Mayor of the Borough was Richard Matthews, seen here with his wife, Judith, the Mayoress. Elected to the Council as a Conservative member in 1983, when his occupation was Chief Cashier at Staveley Chemicals, Richard served on all the committees of the council, his particular interests being recreation and leisure, and the environment. His chosen charity in his Mayoral term of office was the Ashgate Hospice and his efforts resulted in the highest return for a Mayor's Appeal of over £37,000. He now works for the hospice in a fund-raising capacity.

Below: Police matters. The County Police Sports Club tug-of-war section at their second annual dinner at the Queen's Head Hotel in the early 1950s. They displayed their three trophies, won in the first year of their formation. Standing, left to right: Insp. F.E.K. Pegg, Cons. J. Hinchley, Cons. H. Martin, D.C. Stockley, Sgt J.K. Carberry, Ex-Cons. W.S. Buck, Cons. A. Farquhar, D.Cons. G.W. Stephen, Cons. A. Amedro, Cons. R. Twigg, Insp. T.A. Basnett. Seated: Insp. T.A. Merchant, Supt. A. Rudin, Supt. J. Davies, Supt. J. Austin, Supt. T.S. Wright, Mr E.R.L. Powell, C.Insp. W.A. Sheffield.

The long-awaited Museum of Chesterfield finally opened its doors to the public on 13 May 1994, in the west end of the Stephenson Memorial Hall, recently vacated by the Central Library. The opening ceremony, seen here, was performed by Henry Sandon, the well-known pottery expert of Antiques Road Show fame, accompanied by the Mayor and Mayoress, Richard Matthews and his wife, Judith. The museum almost overflows with well-presented exhibits of local interest, supervised by the Curator, Anne-Marie Knowles and her deputy, Roger Shelley.

The Central Library staff grouped at their Christmas party in the old Children's Section, 1951. Front, left to right: Kitty McMahon, Stephanie Horner, John Lilley, Barbara Rawson, Jean Finney and Edna Lenthall. Rear, Roy Cooper, Barbara Attenborough, -?-, Joan Gayles, G.R. Micklewright, Barbara Wagstaffe, Enid Bargh, Janet Bailey, June Fox, Mary Hartley and Keith Wikely.

The St Thomas' Darby and Joan Choir posing outside Bradbury Hall in the early 1970s with some of the many prizes won at festivals. The choir started life in the old St Thomas' school-room and on its closure was found meeting and practice accommodation courtesy of Robinson and Sons. The choir, in those days, numbered twenty eight and was led by Charlie Cooper, with Florence Robinson as president. The average age of the choir members was seventy years.

A band leads the Sunday School of the Storrs Road Methodist Church on their well-supported Whit Walk along Storrs Road in the late 1970s.

The *Derbyshire Times* celebrated its centenary, in February 1954, with a dinner for the staff at the Station Hotel. Posing at the top table, seated, left to right: Mrs T.D. McEwan, Mr J.F. Edmunds (joint managing director), Mrs M.H. Edmunds, Mr G.J. Edmunds (chairman and managing director), Mrs G.J. Edmunds, Mr M.H. Edmunds (editor and joint managing director), Mrs J.F. Edmunds. Standing, left to right: Mr W.R. Wallwork (advertising manager and director), Mr Gordon McEwan, Mr H. Oliver (assistant advertising manager), Miss Susan Edmunds, Mrs L.C. Lowe, Mr L.C. Lowe (secretary and director), Miss G. McEwan, Miss Elizabeth Edmunds, Mr J.N.O. Manners (assistand editor and director), Mr P.J.F. Lowe.

A fourteenth-century malting oven found in 1975 by the Chesterfield Archeological Research Committee when seeking evidence for a Roman fort between the (then) White Swan hotel and Station Road. Described by the Director of Excavations, Terry Courtney, as 'perhaps the best ever excavated', the oven was back-filled and left there. It is now under the car park.

Chesterfield's inner relief road was opened on 25 July 1985 by the Transport Minister Lynda Chalker and completed, ten months ahead of schedule, by Balfour Beatty. The picture shows a parade of old cars which took place four days earlier, the Inner Relief Road Charity Day, and raised over £5,000 for the Nedscan Appeal and Ashgate Hospice. Prizes were presented by Mayor Tom Whyatt and actor/comedian Tony Capstick.

Left: A near-disastrous fire on 22 December 1961, in the north transept of St Mary's, thought to have been started by an electrical fault, was fortunately brought under control in a few hours by the firefighters. Many volunteers rescued valuables from fire and water damage. The main loss was the rare Snetzler organ, but the wooden spire was just saved. Right: A new top being fitted to the Market Hall, just prior to its re-opening in November 1980. Margaret Troop JP, President of the National Market Traders' Federation, performed the opening.

On 7 May 1993, an arsonist started a fire on the upper floor of Littlewood's store, which caused two fatalities and several injuries to shoppers. Some escaped from the store by leaping from windows on to vehicles parked below. The arsonist was caught and jailed.

Six

Schooldays

The 'new wing' of the Chesterfield Grammar School in 1947. Built before the war, this addition to the old school housed the fifth forms on the ground floor and the School of Art on the upper storey.

Form 1A of the Grammar School in 1946, photographed at the clock-tower entrance. The form mistress, left of centre, was Mrs Evelyn Hill, who was also active in public life, serving on parish councils, becoming a JP in 1949 and mayoress in 1966. She died in 1992.

The Grammar School from the south-east in 1952, looking over the Eventide Home gardens from the Technical College. In the centre are the 'wooden huts' then housing the third forms, and behind the tree, the 'tin tabernacles', other long-lived 'temporary' accommodation.

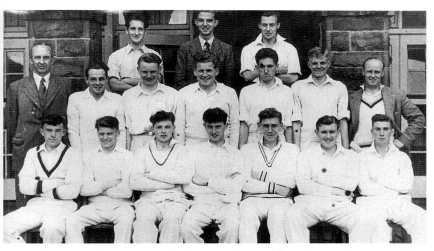

A cricket 1st XI of the Grammar School in 1952 with, rear, left to right: Needham, Frost, Taylor. Centre: W.E. Glister (head), Pexton, Cawley, Smith, Hunt, Evans, Pilkington (master). Front: Cheetham, Farnsworth, Amedro, Jones (captain), Unwin, Austin, Maycock.

The 1st XI football team, posing on the school terrace in 1951-2 with, rear, left to right: W.E. Glister (head), Buchan, Taylor, Needham, Metcalf, Austin, Tillotson, Gordon Jephcote (sports master). Seated: Hooper, Eaton, Hunt (captain), Evans, Peck. The goal-keeper, Metcalfe, later became an Olympic athlete.

The reception classes at Abercrombie Primary School in 1975. The teachers shown with the pupils are Mrs S. Carter (left) and Mrs Hazel Kleesh.

The most recently built school in Chesterfield is St Mary's RC High School at Newbold which was completed in the 1980s. This 1989 photograph shows the sixth forms with senior staff in the centre, left to right: Mr A.D. Whelan (asst. head), Mr J.E. Arrowsmith (head), Sister Brenda O'Brien (snr. mistress) and Mr A. Boardman.

Tapton House from the south in 1968. George Stephenson lived and died in this Georgian mansion and C.P. Markham owned it for some years before giving the estate to the town. It became a co-educational school in 1931, closing as such in the 1980s. It was subsequently converted for use as a college of further education.

Above: A group of senior pupils of Tapton House in 1946. Back row, left to right: F. Kerry, G. Beresford, -?-. Centre row: H. Mellor (head), J. Mitchell, -?-, A. Jones, K. Stockton, P. Morrison, M. Hobson, P. Wildin (snr mistress). Front, seated: J. Welton, J. Croft, S. Renton, M. Pollard, J. Hall, Miss Stanley, J. Orton, B. Nuttall, -?-, J. Fox, B. Cater.

Opposite above: The Tapton House netball team of 1947-8, back row, left to right: Miss Savage, B. Rhodes, L. Paulson, D. Walker, Mr H. Mellor (head). Front: P. Smith, M. Davis, J. Bennett, M. Poll, B. Lord.

Opposite below: This team from Tapton won no less than four trophies in the Secondary Schools Athletics Championships, held in the Queen's Park annexe, in 1966.

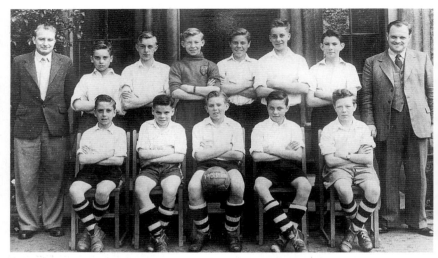

In the 1953-4 football season, Tapton boys were winners too, capturing the Junior Section Clayton Challenge Shield with their under-12 XI, back row, left to right: Mr D.A. Cox, A. Wright, P. Leemort, R. Wilson (later of Arsenal and TV fame), G. Clark, D. Billyeald, I. Collins, Mr A.H. Jennings. Front: L. Garbot, B. Hollis, A.Jackson (captain), A. Bythway, ? Matthews.

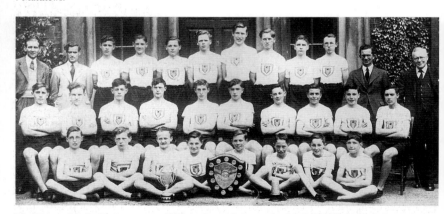

The Tapton boys' athletics team, c. 1948, back row, left to right: Mr S. Haddock, Mr J. Lennon, Barratt, Bramley, Worral, Twelves, Callaghan, Woodhouse, Smith, Marsden, Mr F. Silcock, Mr H. Mellor (head). Centre row: Orwin, Walkley, Lethbridge, Barlow, Bradshaw, Quartermain, Pidcock, Broadhead, Mundy, Bradshaw. Front: Roper, Elliott, Bramley, Walton, Astell, Fane, Key, Hanshaw.

Seven

Small but Interesting

This greetings sign, appropriately cast in iron for a town with three iron-making works, once read 'Welcome to Chesterfield – the centre of industrial England' before the advertisement was added. It used to reside on the A619 at Belmont.

Left: This beautifully executed frontage is on the Punchbowl, Holywell Street and the monogram is that of the Mansfield Brewery. Right: Decorated gables were in fashion at the turn of the twentieth century. This one is on the corner of Packer's Row and High Street and was over Collingwoods when it was photographed.

It is difficult to think of a use other than purely ornamental for this embellishment on the Portland Hotel.

The Portland Hotel again. The frieze over the main entrance carries this plasterwork and is the cannon trademark of William Stones Brewery.

Left: Once a common sight, these bag hoists could be seen on many factories and large shops, where bulk materials were stored on a high floor. This example was photographed in the 1960s on the town side of Brampton Brewery. Right: There are many towers and minarets around the town on buildings of the late nineteenth century. This one was built for the Yorkshire Penny Bank on Central Pavement and is now the Halifax Building Society.

Left: In the 1910s there were high iron railings around St Mary's church-yard and no path through from Holywell Street. The railings have gone but some pillars remain on St Mary's Gate. These pomegranate arms are still there. Right: The stained glass on the east end of the church is admired from within but the beautiful stonework is best seen from outside.

This nicely-fashioned inn sign, photographed from the church tower, reminds customers of the White Swan, the old name for the Avenue.

Well-kept plasterwork and a balustrade with a knob missing, still sits above a shop on the west side of Packer's Row.

Left: This intricately carved pilaster fronts the shop on the north-east part of the market place. Older readers may remember it as the Home and Colonial stores. Right: When the old Britt's shop, in South Street, was refurbished this coat of arms tablet was removed and found to have been mounted upside down! It is still there, but now the right way up. Whose arms bore the bees and chevron is not known.

A mythical, lion-like beast adorns the pediment on the bottom corner of Packer's Row.

A stone carved, merchant-like figure forms the door-heading on the same building as above.

This ornamental pediment can be seen on 100 year old photographs of the north side of Burlington St. It is still there.

Where else would this be carved in stone but the King's Head on Knifesmithgate?

These amusing and decorative panels cover the naked ends of the beams above the colonnaded north side of Knifesmithgate and were freshly gold-leafed a few years ago. This one – Pan and pipes – is adjacent to the recently vacated shop of R.J. Stokes.

For what reason was this cast iron pipe in the wall? The groove at the bottom provides a clue. A long chain was pulled through from the old gasworks on Chatsworth Road, on either side of a large gate, to stop traffic when wagons of coal were being shunted by rail to the works, or for trains of coke leaving. It is still in place in 1996.

A sight like this could not have been seen until the post-war years! A forest of aerials and lights, compressed together with the help of a long-focus camera lens, on Foljambe Road.

Swags and a bare shield on the Parker building on the south side of Vicar Lane.

The Eyre Chapel, a thirteenth-century Roman Catholic place of worship, behind the Nag's Head at Newbold, photographed in the early 1980s before some careful and sensitive restoration began. Owned by the Eyre family from the sixteenth century to the 1940s, it has been used as a cow house and a mortuary in its time. Worship was resumed in the chapel from the 1940s until a new church opened nearby.

Generations of the Eyre family worshipped at the chapel and several were interred in the crypt beneath which has now been sealed. The last interment took place in 1926.

Eight

Aerial Views

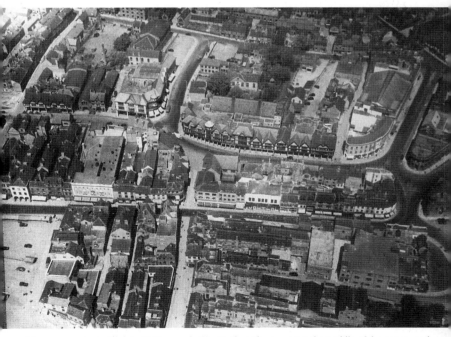

The town centre in the late 1940s or early 50s. Knifesmithgate crosses the middle of the picture and the Co-op has yet to extend the shop to Saltergate. T.P. Woods' colonnade can be seen on the left.

This photograph of the town from Hady Hill, taken in 1985, shows how the town is surrounded by hills. The white scar of the inner relief road is prominent in the morning sun, as is the *Derbyshire Times* works. The background houses are at Holymoorside.

Right: A 1960s view of West Bars and New Square from the Market Hall tower. The new Dent's block is in place but the firm's temporary shop has not yet been removed. The A.G.D. multi-storey park is not yet in position and the Brampton Brewery still survives.

Below: The disused warehouse, yard and offices of Ernest Shentall, fruit and vegetable wholesalers, in 1983. The old white Heathcote house has now had this corrugated roof suitably replaced, has been completely renovated and is a thriving restaurant. The other buildings round the yard have gone and St Mary's Court offices stand here.

Looking west from the church tower in 1983. The old and new rooftops contrast sharply with each other and the image of figures doing the Saturday shopping on a summer's day could almost be a modern picture by Lowry.

This view is thought to be from the 1940s, photographed early on a market day. The still clean looking roof of the Elder Way store of the Co-op contrasts with the grimy market hall.

This view of the town centre from the north-east had been included in my selection for the book before I realised it was recorded late before the last war. I decided to retain it because it is of some interest and probably not many things changed here between 1939 and 1945. The LDEC railway, with its turntable (top left) is active and the market stalls look pretty much as they do today – but how few cars!

A 1974 photograph covering the town centre from the south-east. The new courthouse stands out and also the new car parks in Saltergate but there is no Do-it-All or Pavements mall.

Sheepbridge Works in the late 1950s. Several changes have taken place here since this photograph, looking north-west, was taken. The blast furnaces and associated ancillaries have disappeared and also most of the white heaps of slag. The A61 to Sheffield can clearly be seen, going twice under the Midland Railway line, before approaching Unstone. The Dronfield by-pass is years away.

It is easy to find one's bearings on this 1950s view looking north-west by using the Trebor roof sign. Features that can be seen are the river Rother going under the Brimington road at Tapton Bridge. The old GC (LNER) railway station and loop line are to the centre left and beyond is the old Technical College and Eventide Homes on Infirmary road. The County Court and Police buildings, at the lower right, now house Chesterfield Court business and the Probation Service respectively.

From the church tower looking north. All the Holywell Street shops have changed hands since this 1980s photograph. Tapton Lane is still a through road here and many houses on Durrant Road have disappeared, as have Eyres cabinet factory and the dwellings in Parker's Yard, below the Odeon cinema (left). Trebor has visibly expanded, though, and also the Station Hotel (centre right) but much of this scene was soon to change with the advent of the inner relief road.

There is much detail to see on this 1940s view of lower Brampton from the south. Above the Drill Hall (top right) are Proctor's Ashgate Nurseries and below it are the popular allotments, behind the gas holders. Chatsworth Road slants across the lower part of the photograph, the Mount Zion church prominent with its successive extensions, and the Miners' Welfare, with its tennis courts, can be seen above (centre left).

Another Brampton photograph showing Robinson's mill, in the middle, and Walton dam, just in view bottom left, alongside Walton Road. This crosses the Chatsworth Road where now is sited a roundabout and the Safeway superstore. North of the mill can be seen a couple of old pottery chimneys, either side of Barker Lane, belonging to Barker and Welshpool potteries.

The Boythorpe estate from the west. The long Tube Works mill shed can be seen at the top with the Queen's Park and its annexe alongside and William Rhodes school is just above centre. The layout of the Boythorpe estate is apparent, looking as though an extension westwards was intended but not implemented. The site of the London pottery and brickworks can be seen, lower left, next to Walgrove Road.

A mainly pastoral scene around Walton Road. The golf course is above and, to the side, Foljambe Avenue, a classic ribbon development. The Orchard's Way estate is apparently already marked out.

The Matlock road cuts along the bottom of this view of Walton from the south-west. The 'Blue Stoops' is prominent opposite the Golf Clubhouse.

Western Brampton with St Thomas' church at top right and Storrs Road, upper left. The main line of the trees follows the course of the river Hipper, winding eastwards from Somersall playing-fields, and on the north side of Chatsworth Road is the arc of Vincent Crescent. The open space north, above it, is the site of the present Westfield School. New housing estates now occupy much of the patchwork of allotments below Old Road, at the top of the photograph.